AMAZING ANIMALS

IMPALAS

BY MARI BOLTE

CREATIVE EDUCATION • CREATIVE PAPERBACKS

Published by Creative Education
and Creative Paperbacks
P.O. Box 227, Mankato, Minnesota 56002
Creative Education and Creative Paperbacks
are imprints of The Creative Company
www.thecreativecompany.us

Design by The Design Lab
Production by Blue Design
Art direction by Graham Morgan

Images by Getty Images/Federico Veronesi, 10, Franz Aberham, 18, Mint Images, 14, Paul Souders, 6, Teresa Kopec, 17, WLDavies, 23; Unsplash/Simon Greenwood, 2, Valeria Hutter, cover, 1; Wikimedia Commons/Bernard DUPONT, 8, Biodiversity Heritage Library, 20, Charles J. Sharp, 5, 12, Dietmar Rabich, 13, Giles Laurent, 19, Muhammad Mahdi Karim, 9, 21, Vaughan Leiberum, 16

Cataloging-in-Publication data is available from
the Library of Congress.
Library Binding ISBN: 9798895810552
Paperback ISBN: 9798896800088
eBook ISBN: 9798895811818
LCCN: 2025011358

Printed in China

Table of Contents

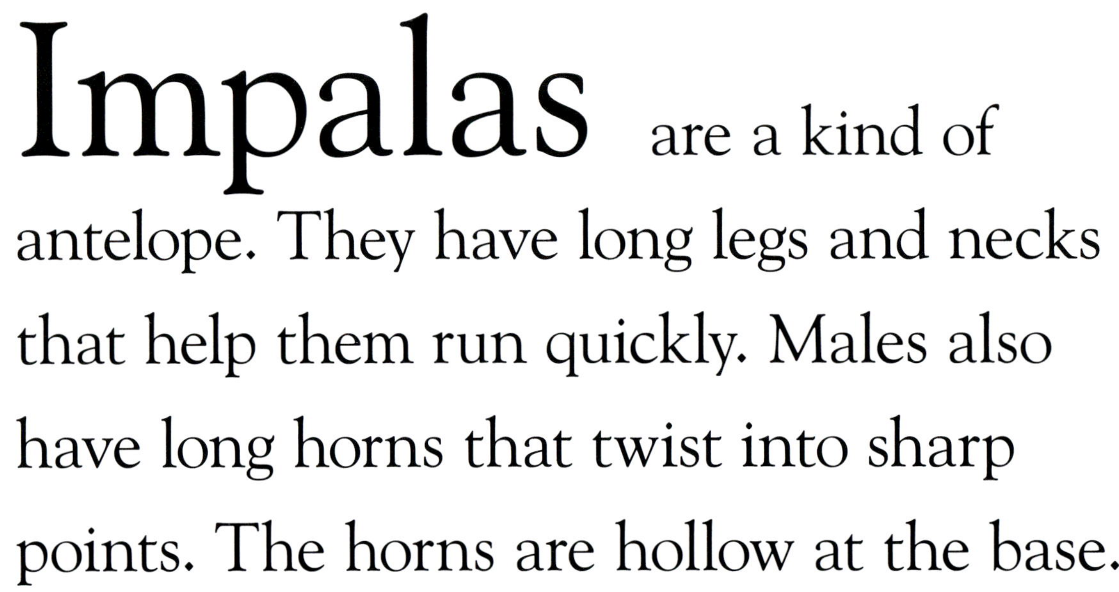

Impalas are a kind of antelope. They have long legs and necks that help them run quickly. Males also have long horns that twist into sharp points. The horns are hollow at the base.

Impalas are also called rooibok. This means "red buck."

Impalas can run 55 miles (90 kilometers) per hour.

Impalas are fast. They jump and run to escape **predators**. Impalas have huge **strides**. They can cover 33 feet (10 meters) with a single bound. They can also hop up to 10 feet (3 m) straight in the air.

predator an animal that eats other animals

stride a long step

Male impalas have scent glands in their foreheads. They rub their heads on trees and plants to tell other males to stay away.

Impalas are not very big. Adults weigh between 88 and 167 pounds (39.9–75.7 kilograms). That is about the size of a large dog. Males are larger than females. However, they all look similar.

gland organ that makes a substance that serves a purpose

Impalas live in eastern and southern Africa. There are many large predators, including lions, cheetahs, and leopards. If an impala senses danger, it makes a loud barking noise. This tells the other impalas to keep watch.

Reddish-brown coats help impalas blend in with their surroundings.

Impalas spend a lot of time grooming themselves and each other.

Impalas are **herbivores**. They eat mainly grass. But they have the most flexible diet of all antelopes. When grass is hard to find, they also eat fruit, leaves, and shrubs. Sharp teeth that can cut plants are also used for grooming. They can comb ticks and other pests out of fur.

herbivore an animal that eats plants

Baby impalas are called fawns. They can be born any time of the year. Pregnant females find a quiet place to give birth to a single fawn. Staying in forests or brushy areas keeps the new fawn safe. After a few days, mother and baby return to the herd.

Impalas usually give birth during the rainy season. There is more grass to eat and places to hide.

Young impalas play together in groups called creches. They stay with their mothers for four to six months. After a year, they are considered adults. Young males make new herds together. Females may stay with their mother or find a new herd too. Herds can have as many as 100 members.

Wild impalas can live up to 15 years. They may live longer in captivity.

Gazelle

Gazelles and impalas look similar. They are both antelopes. There are key differences, though. Gazelles are smaller, and both males and females have horns. There are 17 different species of gazelle. But there is only one species of impala!

The name impala comes from a Zulu word that means gazelle. Are you confused yet?

Around two million impalas live in Africa. They are the most common type of antelope on the continent. Modern-day antelopes are nearly identical to their relatives that lived more than five million years ago. They're perfect the way they are!

Impalas are the main source of food for many predators.

An Impala Story

Hyena was hungry. He watched Mother Impala with her baby and saw an easy meal. He ran toward them. To his surprise, mother and baby ran in different directions! Hyena chased the mother but never caught her. Next, he looked for the baby. It had found its father! Hyena looked at Father Impala's sharp horns. Hyena sighed. He would have to find something else to eat.

Read More

Howell, Izzi. *Animal Athletes*. New York: Crabtree Publishing Company, 2020.

Hughes, Catherine D. *Little Kids First Big Book of African Animals.* Washington, D.C.: National Geographic Kids, 2025.

Websites

Britannica Kids: Impala
https://kids.britannica.com/kids/article/impala/602059
Learn more about these speedy creatures.

World Animal Foundation: Impala
https://worldanimalfoundation.org/advocate/wild-animals/params/post/1291286/impalas
Read fascinating facts about an amazing animal.

Note: Every effort has been made to ensure that the websites listed above are suitable for children, that they have educational value, and that they contain no inappropriate material. However, because of the nature of the Internet, it is impossible to guarantee that these sites will remain active indefinitely or that their contents will not be altered.

Index